To: _____

From: _____

Published by Cumberland House Publishing, an imprint of Sourcebooks, Inc.
P.O. Box 4410, Naperville, Illinois 60567–4410
(630) 961–3900
Fax: (630) 961–2168
www.sourcebooks.com

Printed and bound in China
OGP 10 9 8 7 6 5 4 3

Why A Daughter Needs A Dad

Coupons

GREGORY E. LANG

CUMBERLAND HOUSE

A daughter needs a dad

to teach her that her role in a family
is greater than the work she does.

Set other plans aside; this entitles us to an hour of quality time together.

A daughter needs a dad

to be the safe spot she can always turn to.

Dad, you've always been there for me, and I'm there for you too.
Good for a phone date whenever you want.

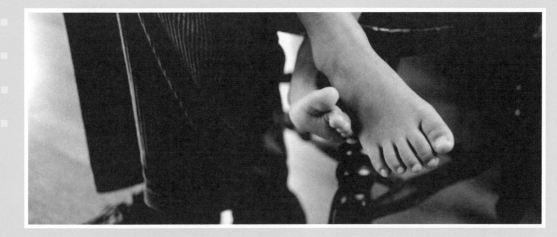

A daughter needs a dad

to be the history of her family for her own children.

Share your stories with me. I promise to listen
whether I've heard them before or not.

A daughter needs a dad

to teach her when to be firm and when to compromise.

This time, you get the last word:
Good for winning one argument, no contest.

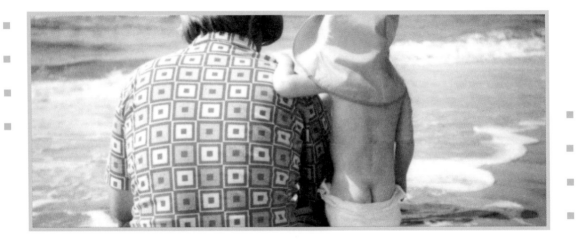

A daughter needs a dad

to calm her when she is stressed by her challenges.

Now it's your turn. Good for one hour of uninterrupted relaxation.

A daughter needs a dad

who teaches her she is important by stopping
what he is doing to watch her.

Dad, you're important to me too. I'll make dinner for you tonight—your pick.

A daughter needs a dad

to teach her how things work.

Dad, you've always helped me out. Redeem this when you
need *me* to teach *you* something.

A daughter needs a dad

to protect her from thunder and lightning.

Rainy Day Coupon: Even though it's dreary outside, let's make
hot cocoa and watch your favorite movie.

A daughter needs a dad

to teach her not to let pride get in the way of discovering new things.

Let's go to a new restaurant you want to try—my treat.

A daughter needs a dad

to teach her how to focus her mind
in the midst of distraction.

Let me help you focus: Good for one evening of peace and quiet.

A daughter needs a dad

to remind her of what she may not remember.

Good for an evening of looking through photo albums and reminiscing together.

A daughter needs a dad

to teach her the joy of serving others.

Today we'll help others by volunteering at the charity of your choice.

A daughter needs a dad

to show her that true love is unconditional.

I love you, Dad. Good for one big hug whenever you need it.

A daughter needs a dad

to teach her that loving her family is a priority.

Today we will make time to talk to each other,
no matter the subject or how long it takes.

A daughter needs a dad

who will never think she is too old to need him.

I always need you, Dad. Will you help me out today?

A daughter needs a dad

to teach her to learn from her experiences.

Let's learn from an experience together today. Museum, sporting event, or even just talking together—your pick!

A daughter needs a dad

to help her find her way in life.

You choose the trail this weekend—let's go for a walk or hike together.

A daughter needs a dad

who does not mind when she steps on his shoes while dancing.

I always have fun dancing with you, Dad. Let's put on some music and go crazy!

A daughter needs a dad

to show her the benefits of hard work.

Here's a sweet benefit from a little work: Redeem for one batch of freshly baked cookies.

A daughter needs a dad

to teach her to spend responsibly, save for a rainy day, and give with a generous heart.

I've been saving up, Dad—today I'm taking you out!

A daughter needs a dad

to help her finish her work when she is too weary to finish it herself.

Dad, it's my turn to help you finish your work. Relax—I'll do a chore you dread for the whole week.

A daughter needs a dad

who will laugh at her at all the right times.

Let's share a laugh together and watch our favorite funny movie.